P9-BYE-826

PROJECT SEEK - PRE - K
AT RISK GRANT
ROCKFORD, ILLINOIS

Who Uses This?

by Margaret Miller

Greenwillow Books, New York

I would like to thank all of the following children, grown-ups, and organizations whose patience, generosity, and good humor made this book possible: Allan Kerr, Sabrina Steel, Rebecca Chace, Sam Spector, the Columbia University Department of Athletics, Michael Fusco, Diana Lizardi, Sylvia Roberts, the Bank Street College Cafeteria, Mika Sneddon, Eliza Reed of Wave Hill, Peter Concannon, Lydia and Andrew Devine, Mitch Miller and the Rochester Philharmonic Orchestra, Desmond Maxwell, Ruth Hoffman, Jamie Tate, Gerry Gilfedder of Delta Hair Stylists, Tommy Zipser, Georgia Warner, Chuck and Maggie Close, and Hannah Spector.

Copyright © 1990 by Margaret Miller. All rights reserved. No part of this book may be reproduced or utilized in any form or by any means, electronic or mechanical, including photocopying, recording, or by any information storage and retrieval system, without permission in writing from the Publisher, Greenwillow Books, a division of William Morrow & Company, Inc., 105 Madison Avenue, New York, NY 10016. Printed in Singapore by Tien Wah Press. First Edition 10 9 8 7 6 5 4 3 2 1

Library of Congress Cataloging-in-Publication Data

Miller, Margaret (date)
Who uses this? / Margaret Miller.
p. cm.
Summary: Brief text, in question and answer form,
and accompanying photographs introduce a variety
of objects, their purpose, and who uses them.
ISBN 0-688-08278-5. ISBN 0-688-08279-3 (lib. bdg.)
1. Tools—Miscellanea—Juvenile literature.
2. Occupations—Miscellanea—Juvenile literature.
[1. Tools. 2. Occupations. 3. Questions and
answers.]
I. Title. TT153.M48 1990
331.7′02—dc20 89-30456 CIP AC

For my father,
with admiration and love

Who uses this?

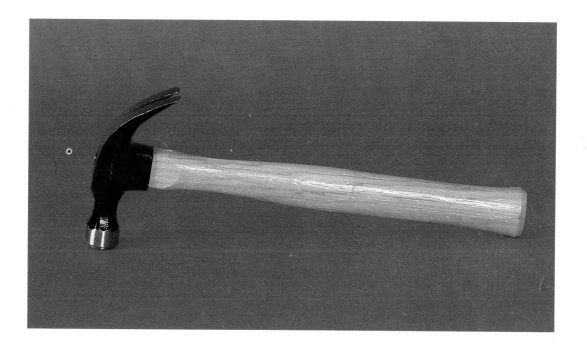

Carpenter

Who uses this?

Juggler

Who uses this?

Football player

Who uses this?

Baker

Who uses this?

Gardener

Who uses this?

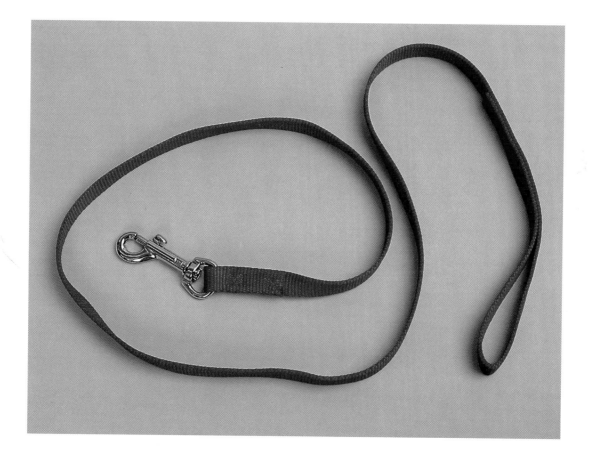

Dog walker

Who uses this?

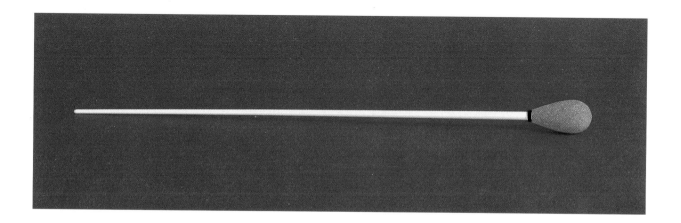

Conductor

Who uses this?

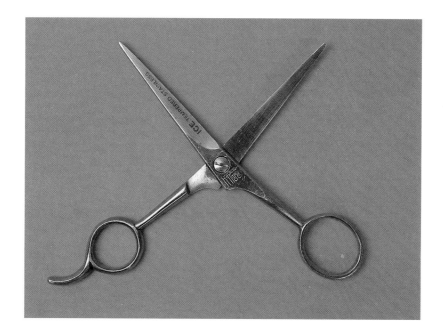

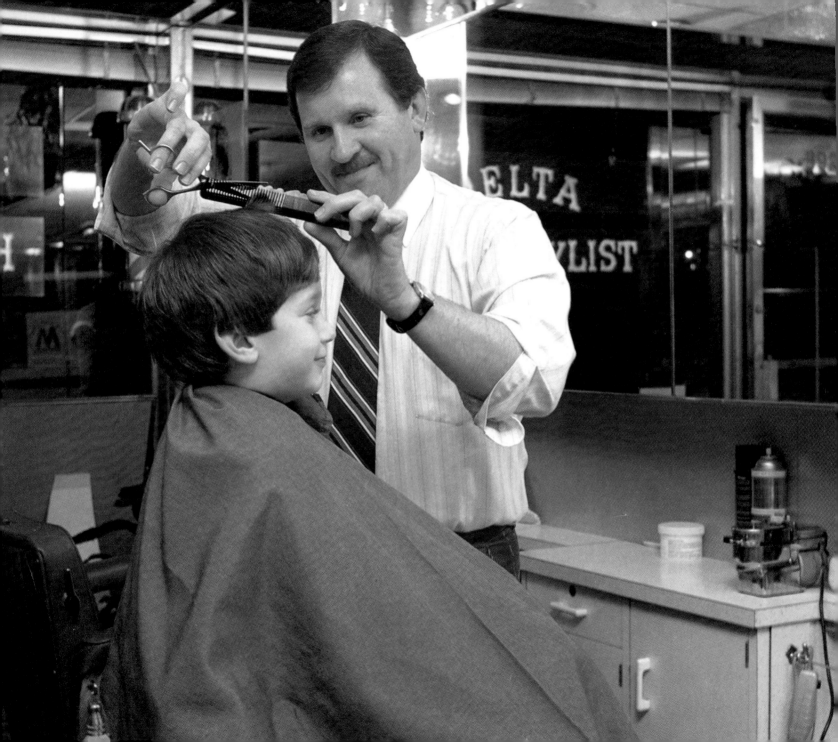

Barber

Who uses this?

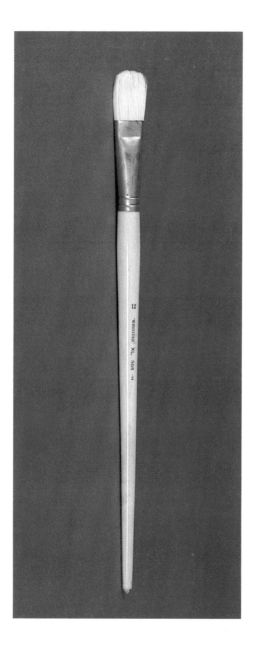

Artist

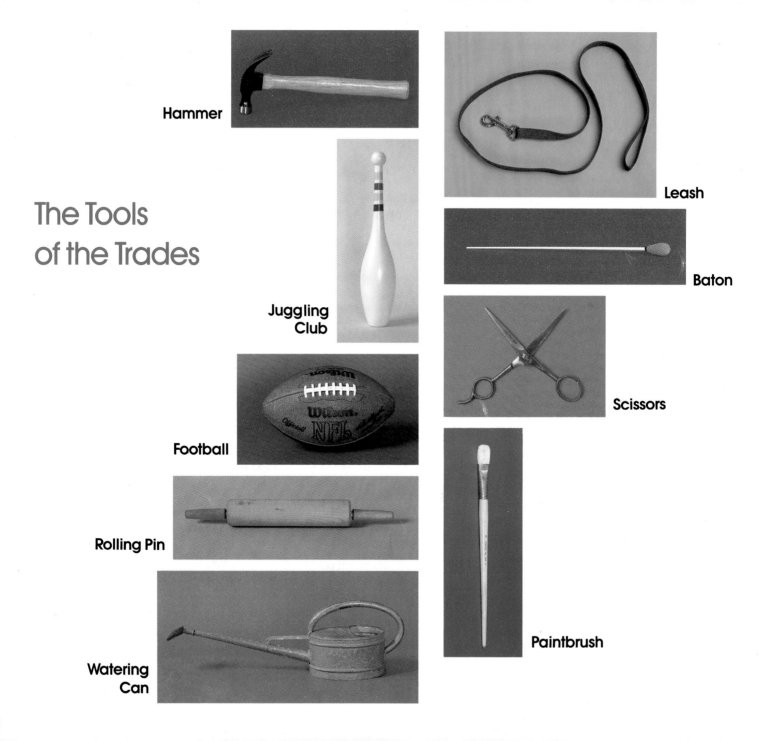

The Tools
of the Trades

Hammer

Leash

Juggling
Club

Baton

Football

Scissors

Rolling Pin

Watering
Can

Paintbrush